IN THE
NATIONAL INTEREST

General Sir John Monash once exhorted a graduating class to 'equip yourself for life, not solely for your own benefit but for the benefit of the whole community'. At the university established in his name, we repeat this statement to our own graduating classes, to acknowledge how important it is that common or public good flows from education.

Universities spread and build on the knowledge they acquire through scholarship in many ways, well beyond the transmission of this learning through education. It is a necessary part of a university's role to debate its findings, not only with other researchers and scholars, but also with the broader community in which it resides.

Publishing for the benefit of society is an important part of a university's commitment to free intellectual inquiry. A university provides civil space for such inquiry by its scholars, as well as for investigations by public intellectuals and expert practitioners.

This series, In the National Interest, embodies Monash University's mission to extend knowledge and encourage informed debate about matters of great significance to Australia's future.

Professor Margaret Gardner AC
President and Vice-Chancellor,
Monash University

CARRILLO GANTNER

DISMAL DIPLOMACY, DISPOSABLE SOVEREIGNTY: OUR PROBLEM WITH CHINA & AMERICA

MONASH
UNIVERSITY
PUBLISHING

Monash University Publishing
Matheson Library Annexe
40 Exhibition Walk
Monash University
Clayton, Victoria 3800, Australia
https://publishing.monash.edu

Monash University Publishing brings to the world publications which advance the best traditions of humane and enlightened thought.

ISBN: 9781922633149 (paperback)
ISBN: 9781922633163 (ebook)

Series: In the National Interest
Editor: Louise Adler
Project manager & copyeditor: Paul Smitz
Designer: Peter Long
Typesetter: Cannon Typesetting
Proofreader: Gillian Armitage
Printed in Australia by Ligare Book Printers

A catalogue record for this book is available from the National Library of Australia.

DISMAL DIPLOMACY, DISPOSABLE SOVEREIGNTY: OUR PROBLEM WITH CHINA & AMERICA

Australia's current relationship with China is built on a lie in which ideology has overpowered reality. It is true that China has in recent times been behaving towards Australia like a schoolyard bully picking on small fry. Our current political leaders think it is fine to poke the bully in the eye and call him names when our big protector, Uncle Sam, is also in the yard telling us to do so, but whose national interest is being served by our continuing provocation? Are we not thinking clearly because we are so used to being told how to behave and what to do? Why can't we grow up and be a modern, independent Australia, confident in our own identity?

Australia today should be enjoying a respectful, active and mutually beneficial relationship with China, one that builds on forty years of investment in almost every area of our national life, from politics, business, education, tourism, science and technology, to cultural exchange, law and agriculture—a relationship that has enormously enriched Australia and its people financially, socially, culturally and in so many other ways.

THE POWER OF FUSION

In 1980, when the Nanjing Acrobatic Troupe was set to do a matinee at the Palais Theatre in Melbourne, I invited the first crop of children from the recently formed Flying Fruit Fly Circus to come down from Albury–Wodonga to see the show, and afterwards to come onstage to meet the artists and see their specialist props—the trick bicycles, the teeterboards, the hoops, poles, leather straps and tower of chairs used by artists of huge physical strength, discipline, courage and flexibility to amaze and delight. The kids were boggle-eyed with excitement. My own six-year-old son was there too. The Nanjing performers jested that they wanted to take him home with them because he was exactly the right age to begin the extensive and tough training in China for a career as a top acrobat.

On that day at the Palais, the idea came to me to bring some of these artists who were at the very top of their profession, among the best in the world, back to Australia to train our young people, to create a career path in specialist physical acrobatic and circus skills, a path that simply did not exist in Australia at that time. Both the Australia Council for the Arts and the Chinese Ministry of Culture initially thought this was an extremely stupid idea—they said we had no acrobatic tradition, that our kids wouldn't be interested, that they couldn't speak Chinese etc. It took three years, countless meetings in both countries, and ultimately a show of courage and trust from government and private funders to give it a go. The first $5000 of support for this project came from the Australia–China Council, which had been established by the federal government in 1978 to promote mutual understanding and encourage people to seek engagement between Australia and China. As is so often still the case, other support followed this modest tick of government backing.

In late 1983, seven members of the Nanjing Acrobatic Troupe returned to Australia to work with the Flying Fruit Fly Circus, Circus Oz and a range of independent theatre artists over three months of harshly intensive training. We chose to run the program in Albury–Wodonga not only because it was the Fruit Flies' base, but also, and more importantly, so that it could operate within the embrace of a small and welcoming community without metropolitan distractions. The Chinese trainers were initially shocked by the very low technical skill base of the raw young Australians who were more focused on community and ideological outcomes than on high personal achievement. With an extraordinary commitment from both sides, however, the training culminated in an ecstatic performance at the end of February 1984 which we cheekily titled 'The Great Leap Forward'. And for every artist involved, and for Australian contemporary circus, acrobatics and physical theatre, it truly was. Indeed, the program was so wildly successful that it was repeated the following summer, again for three intense months.

You can trace the establishment of the National Institute of Circus Arts (NICA) at Swinburne University in Melbourne directly back to the Nanjing Acrobatic Training Program. From those first young participants, you can now track at least two generations of top Australian physical performers whose highly trained bodies and disciplined minds have formed the core of their success. You can draw a line from Nanjing to the national and international success of Australian physical theatre—Circus Oz, Circa, the Flying Fruit Flies, Acrobat, Legs on the Wall, Rock 'n' Roll Circus, Gravity & Other Myths, Strut 'n' Fret Productions, Stalker, Dislocate, Strange Fruit, Cirkidz Inc, the Women's Circus, Circus Monoxide, and many, many other companies, small ensembles and individual artists from every state and territory. I see them and I know their genetic inheritance from Chinese training methods, professional prowess and pride, married to Australian production values, political irreverence and community connection. This has bred an exciting new hybrid, a recognisably Australian style now celebrated around the world—a very rich legacy indeed of deep Australia–China cultural sharing and exchange.

Soft you; a word or two before you go.
I have done the state some service, and they know't.

Othello, Act 5, Scene 2

THE CREATIVE ROAD TO BEIJING

I first became interested in China as an under-graduate at Melbourne University in the early 1960s. Myra Roper, a China scholar, author, and the principal of what was then University Women's College (now simply University College), was a close friend of my mother's and often at our home talking encouragingly about developments in the People's Republic. When I returned to Australia in 1969 from graduate studies in drama at Stanford University in California—initially to work at the Adelaide Festival and then as the first drama officer at the new Australia Council for the Arts—I joined the Committee for a New China Policy, an informal lobby group led by Stephen FitzGerald and Myra Roper. Its aim was to encourage our then federal government to give diplomatic recognition to the People's Republic of China (PRC) rather than maintain the absurd fiction that the Kuomintang government isolated in Taiwan was the real admin-istrator of the massive landmass and population of mainland China.

I first travelled to China in February 1977 with a delegation from this group, which had been renamed the Committee for Australia–China Relations after prime minister Gough Whitlam had announced on 5 December 1972, his first day in office, that Australia would recognise the PRC. We had intended to visit in October the previous year, but a day before we were due to leave, the Chinese Embassy in Canberra had cancelled the trip. In retrospect, it was clear that they had either been told that Mao Zedong was already dead or that he was about to die, because the next day, news of his passing sped around the world.

As a founding director of Melbourne's Playbox Theatre Company, I led the first Australian theatre group to travel to China in 1978 at the invitation of the Chinese Ministry of Culture. The following year, I presented the superlative glove puppetry masters from the Fujian Puppet Theatre of China to great acclaim and a sold-out season at the Playbox Theatre in Exhibition Street, Melbourne, and subsequently in Sydney. It was as a result of this success that, in 1980, I was invited by the Chinese Embassy to take the fifty-member Nanjing Acrobatic Troupe on a six-week tour around the mainland state capital cities plus Canberra.

The Playbox Theatre board said this was way too big an operation for our little company to manage on its own—the budget for the tour of over $1 million even then was about twice our annual budget—so I invited my friend, the distinguished Australian theatre promoter Clifford Hocking, to join us. To protect our respective bases from the financial risks involved in a major commercial tour, we established a separate company, Playking Productions Pty Ltd, to manage the event. Playking was 50 per cent owned by PLAYbox and 50 per cent by Clifford HocKING. We thought that this was much more felicitous than the alternative 'Hockbox', and it sounded rather Chinese, like Peking, Nanking and Chongking. Clifford and I went to Nanjing in late 1979 to arrange the program, and the following year, as the production's national tour director, I flew to Hong Kong to collect the troupe for their six weeks on the road, opening in Perth.

We followed this in 1983 with another six-week, fifty-member national tour by the Jiangsu Peking Opera Company, offering two programs of different extracts from this spectacular form of theatre. This time we invited The Australian Elizabethan Theatre Trust and promoter Michael Edgley to join us as investing partners, and again I went on the road as tour director while Clifford and his partner David Vigo managed the budgets and marketing from their Melbourne office. To everyone's amazement, this gruelling outing of classical Chinese opera played very successfully in major theatres in each state capital—the tour even made a very small profit.

The large acrobatic and opera companies both came from Jiangsu Province, of which Nanjing is the capital. Why from there? Because Victoria and Jiangsu had become sister states in 1979 under the enthusiastic shepherding of our then Liberal premier Sir Rupert Hamer, who presciently saw the enormous opportunities for expanded trade, education and cultural exchange with China. In 1983, Playbox Theatre also presented the Hunan Puppet Company—this one a rod-puppet group— at St Martin's Theatre in Melbourne.

Each of the aforementioned Chinese companies offered exposure to exquisite artistry that had been handed down through generations, and performance forms that were new to Australian artists and audiences. They offered windows into the rich and ancient cultural traditions of an old civilisation, broadening our horizons and adding new colours to the creative and contemporary multicultural tapestry we were striving to weave here in Australia.

It was especially gratifying to see our audiences so excited by the talent of these fine companies, and they left a variety of legacies. Beautifully costumed puppets from both the Fujian and Hunan puppet companies were gifted into the Performing Arts Collection housed at Arts Centre Melbourne. In 1989 I brought back to Melbourne two of the senior Jiangsu Peking Opera artists to introduce this symbolic and non-naturalistic form to drama students at the Victorian College of the Arts. I was not looking to produce local Peking opera stars, but rather to give the students a different vocabulary of performance that might enrich their own continuing practice. Peking opera is so utterly different to contemporary naturalistic Western drama: a plain table and two chairs can symbolise the world; a long journey is represented by the actor circling the stage, with a tasselled whip indicating that a horse is providing the transportation; a yellow silk robe embroidered with a five-toed dragon shows the character's imperial status.

As I described earlier, the impact of the Nanjing Acrobatic Training Program on Australian circuses, acrobatics, physical theatre, and indeed on the performing arts more generally, has been profound and positive. In terms of the personal legacy he has shared with us all, I pay special tribute to the great performer who did breathtaking handstands atop a tower of chairs, the program's master instructor, Lu Guang Rong. After the second Nanjing program, Mr Lu remained in Australia as a superlative performer and teacher, first at the Flying Fruit Fly Circus and then, after NICA opened in 2000, as head of teaching there for another fifteen years. As he so richly deserved, Mr Lu was honoured with a Medal of the Order of Australia in 2015.

In late 1984, I was invited to apply for the position of cultural counsellor at the Australian Embassy in Beijing. While I had good contacts in the Ministry of Culture in that city and in some of the provincial cultural bureaux, and very strong on-the-ground experience in promoting cultural relations with China, I still think the Department of Foreign Affairs made a brave choice when appointing me, a theatre professional, to the role rather than a career diplomat, as my three fine predecessors after 1972 had been—Dr Jocelyn Chey, Ross Maddock and Sam Gerovich. After several months of basic language training, which was totally insufficient, I travelled to Beijing to take up the position, in April 1985.

Apart from the first three months of my posting, the Australian ambassador during my three years in Beijing was the brilliant Professor Ross Garnaut, previously senior economic adviser to prime minister Bob Hawke. Because, like me, Ross was not a career foreign affairs officer, he was not so concerned with diplomatic niceties but rather with results. I was encouraged to go forth and expand Australia's cultural engagement with the assurance that I had the ambassador's full support—and behind him, that of the prime minister. I soon became aware that my brief was expansive. Apart from culture in the artistic sense, and sport, which is a dynamic part of the Australian ethos, I was also responsible for the programs of the Australia–China Council; for academic exchanges; for science, technology and medicine; for conservation and the environment; for law and accounting; for the Australian students in China (although not the Chinese students just beginning to go to Australia); even for agriculture, the only logic being the spelling, as I used to joke; indeed, for anything that came to the embassy that was not politics, trade, aid or defence.

All of these roles gave me opportunities for travel around China, and I made the most of them. A few of the wonderful experiences I had were negotiating the year-long visit of two giant pandas which came to Melbourne and Sydney for the Bicentenary in 1988; travelling to Tibet to prepare the way, like John the Baptist, for Susan Ryan's proposed first coming in her role as minister for education; accompanying minister for science Barry Jones to Xichang, China's rocket-launching base in Sichuan Province, when he was exploring the use of Chinese facilities to put Australia's first-generation AUSSAT communication satellites into orbit; twice accompanying former prime minister Whitlam around China in his capacity as chairman of the Australia–China Council, on one occasion taking notes for his meeting with Deng Xiaoping in Beijing's Great Hall of the People; negotiating the annual exchange program under the bilateral Cultural Agreement; and attending 187 performances of Chinese opera, drama, acrobatics, dance and film, plus those of many wonderful visiting companies, including our own Australian Ballet whose tour in 1986 I negotiated.

It was a golden time in the Sino-Australian relationship, with China opening itself up to the world and both sides keen to deepen the relationship and learn from each other. In Chinese Government agencies, artistic circles and academia, everyone was welcoming and supportive.

A STRETCH OF THE DIPLOMATIC IMAGINATION

One of my responsibilities as cultural counsellor was to try to make sense of what I was seeing and hearing and to write reports for Foreign Affairs that attempted to analyse the significance of this not only in the cultural dimension but also the political. It sometimes surprised my colleagues in the political section of the embassy that I was able to detect trends before they did. This was simply because, in China, culture is very close to ideology and the winds of political change are frequently felt first on artists' cheeks. In China, as in every Asian country I know, culture is placed at the very centre of life through a broad understanding of one's language, history, education, art, food, even politics, whereas in Australia many people still seem to think culture is what you do on Saturday night.

The arts in Australia are not generally thought to be a measure of society, a powerful force for social cohesion and economic betterment. Here, if the government thinks of the arts at all, it is usually either in terms of froth and celebrity, especially in relation to film and television, or as a left-wing cabal. Conservative federal governments have not even thought it necessary or beneficial to have a national cultural policy. But in China, I've found that the hopes we express as artists in Australia, about art influencing society, are experienced for real. China's tight political censorship across the arts is paradoxically a compliment to the power of creative practice, a show of respect for the influence that art can have across society.

A personal highlight of my time in China, because it took me back to my role as an artist, as opposed to my role as a foreign affairs bureaucrat, was directing Jack Hibberd's *A Stretch of the Imagination* for the Shanghai People's Art Theatre. The invitation came from the company's artistic director, the controversial playwright Sha Yexin, after I had been vetted in an interview with the grand old man of modern spoken drama (*hua ju*) in China, Huang Zuolin. While my working as a director was acceptable to the Ministry of Culture, which was aware of my background as an actor and director in Australian professional theatre, it was initially disallowed by the Ministry of Foreign Affairs, which decided that a diplomat could not be permitted to stray outside the customary boundaries. We resolved this in an eminently pragmatic Chinese way—I handed in my diplomatic passport, with its special government status and privileges, and I became a visiting artist, using my ordinary passport for the period of the rehearsals and performance.

I offered to the company several plays for which I had commissioned translations and from which they might choose. I expected their choice would be Ray Lawler's classic *Summer of the Seventeenth Doll* because its formal structure was not dissimilar to the works of the famous modern Chinese playwright Cao Yu. Instead, they chose Jack Hibberd's colourful and significant work—titled *Xiang Ru Fei Fei* in Pinyin—for the simple reason that they had never done a one-man play before. (Why would you when your company has over 150 actors on the payroll, which is not counting the many other no-longer-active artists whose retirement benefits you also meet.) They cast a wonderful character actor, Wei Zongwan, in the role of Monk O'Neil, a cantankerous old outback philosopher who goes about his daily chores while re-enacting moments drawn from his past as he waits to die with the going down of the sun.

I had two translations of *Stretch* prepared by Professor Hu Wenzhong, director of the Australian Studies Centre at Beijing Foreign Studies University, who had an MA in Australian Literature from Sydney University under Professor Leonie Kramer, and who understood our Aussie idiom. One was exactly literal, trying to capture the precise meaning and colour (often blue, or 'yellow' as the Chinese would say) of Hibberd's extravagant language. The second tried to replace the wilder idiom—for instance, 'You two-timing fuck-witted mongrel of a slut'—with recognisable Chinese phrases of comparable force but without the superfluous offence, so that audiences could feel more attuned to the flavour of the work.

We rehearsed mornings and late afternoons in a studio at the Shanghai Drama Academy.

During the three-hour lunch break, I rode my bike to the Australian Consulate General, where I acted as unofficial consul general because we happened to be between incumbents at the time. In the rehearsal room I had a full-time interpreter by my side who could explain the complexities of language and meaning, but we quickly found that the actor could best understand my direction around the character's physical expression when I acted it out myself on the floor. The Chinese have a wonderful sense of humour and this aspect of O'Neil's character, as well as his pathos, was frequently understood without words.

About ten days before the opening, all the senior leaders in the company, and one or two people I didn't know, came into the rehearsal room to watch a run-through. I was then put through a rigorous but respectful session of 'criticism and self-criticism', which was tough to absorb yet tremendously valuable, not only in improving the production but also in helping me learn something about humility. All of us are good at giving criticism but not so good at receiving it. Honest self-criticism is even harder, and correspondingly more powerful. Our politicians could try it.

Just before we were to open at the Lyceum Theatre, situated across the road from the Jin Jiang Hotel in central Shanghai, the city's Cultural Bureau declared the production '*Nei Bu*'. Essentially, this meant that the work was thought to be offensive or otherwise problematic, and that therefore only members of the Communist Party could see the show—they were thought to possess sufficiently strong moral fibre to be able to resist the play's negative influence. The general public, on the other hand, would not be allowed to buy tickets.

The minister (or number 2) in our embassy, David Ambrose, flew down to Shanghai to support me. He and I took the senior officials of the Cultural Bureau to a long lunch, and a box office disaster was thereby averted. One of the two offending moments in the production seemed to be the actor's simulated but utterly convincing urination into a barrel. The other was a florid line in the script which was followed by the words, 'Homer said that.' The translator, Professor Hu, had used the common transliteration for the classical Greek writer's name, 'He Ma.' In other tones, this meant 'hippopotamus', which, unbeknown to us, had been street slang for the ageing Mao Zedong before he'd died ten years earlier.

Inadvertently, we were sending up the god-like figure of the late chairman. A courteous willingness to understand the issues from the Chinese perspective and to explain our position respectfully meant that all restrictions were lifted and the production was allowed to proceed without change.

Both aforementioned moments drew gasps and embarrassed giggles from the audience every night. The other thing I recall vividly about the audience reaction was the confusion that arose from the idea that one person could live by themselves in a vast expanse far removed from any other people. In a country of well over a billion people, and not least in crowded Shanghai, the very idea was patently weird and difficult to comprehend.

I loved working in Shanghai. To my mind it is the most dynamic metropolitan centre on earth, as New York must have been in the first half of the twentieth century; and like New York, you can find whatever you want from anywhere on earth somewhere in the city. I loved the daily creative stimulation of cross-cultural rehearsals, and I look back on this experience as one of the very happiest and most satisfying couple of months in my life. But life goes on.

CHEERLEADERS FOR CONTAINMENT

After three years spent living in China, mostly in Beijing, I returned to Australia, to the Playbox Theatre Company where I was artistic director, and then to other roles such as chairman of The Asialink Centre at the University of Melbourne, president of Arts Centre Melbourne, and chairman of the Melbourne International Arts Festival, as well as a continuing involvement in, and support for, cultural exchange that kept me linked in various ways to the ongoing challenges of our relationship with China. Does that qualify me to comment on the current political impasse with the PRC? To quote Shakespeare again:

> I am in blood
> Stepped in so far, that, should I wade no more,
> Returning were as tedious as go o'er.
> Macbeth, Act 4, Scene 3

The tragedy of the recent and very rapid collapse of Australia's good bilateral relations with China is our failure to recognise our wilful infliction of self-harm.

Earlier Australian prime ministers accepted, and sometimes touted, Australia's support for American military containment of China in the Pacific. We never said this openly, of course, but we did allow president Barack Obama to announce the so-called US Pacific 'Pivot' in our own parliament, which involved Australian Government approval for the rotation of US Marines on a base just outside Darwin. We had been told what Obama was going to say, but we didn't even think it might be necessary, or courteous, to inform our regional neighbours, especially Indonesia, that a US base was being established on their doorstep. Now we are repeating that pattern of behaviour, trumpeting the Quad (Quadrilateral Security Dialogue) which, for all the obfuscation of language, is simply another grouping designed to contain China. Successive prime ministers on both sides of domestic politics have utterly failed to give us an assessment of what it might mean for Australia to pick sides in a great-power strategic rivalry in the Pacific.

I would argue that this is not our contest, and that America's national interest is not exactly the same as Australia's national interest. We want a very good relationship with the United States, but we should not have to give this up to have a strong, courteous and workmanlike relationship with China. Unfortunately, Malcolm Turnbull seemed to go out of his way to offend the Chinese, and then our current Prime Minister, who fell into the job with no knowledge or experience of China whatsoever, accepted without question the Trumpish view of China as the enemy, turning on its head the previous forty years of bipartisan national investment in building strong and positive relations. Just as China told us, if we treat them as the enemy, we should not be surprised if they behave as such.

China's power is growing, as is its assertion of that power under President Xi Jinping. We see reports of the repression of the Uyghur population in Xinjiang in the name of fighting terrorism. We see the application of national security legislation in Hong Kong—although from the Chinese perspective, this is doing no more than Western governments do to ensure the stability and safety of their citizens, remembering that Hong Kong is again part of the PRC and not a British war trophy or colonial outpost. We may not like this behaviour, but it actually does not threaten us or the international community any more than other significant current examples of repression across the world to which we regularly turn a blind eye, such as occurs in Belarus or Saudi Arabia or via the confinement of two million Palestinians in the Gaza Strip.

We do not have to like its form of government to deal with China in a more informed and balanced way.

Every day we are bombarded with negative views of China by members of the government and the mainstream Australian media, not least by the Murdoch press, but even regularly by the ABC. Murdoch's Sky News shares the far-right nastiness of America's Fox News along with an overload of anti-China narratives. Almost every story is distorted and simplified with the pejorative and monotonous label of 'communist'—'the communist government', 'a communist front organisation', 'communist-controlled', 'communist influence and infiltration'—as though this word, all by itself, explains the threat, the subterfuge, the corruption, the disappointment, and as though this word alone justifies our hostility. Say the magic word 'communist' and apparently, all by itself, this explains why the Chinese Government is being so unreasonable in its demands that Australia should treat it with the same respect and courtesy we give to other countries with whom we want strong trading relations.

The Chinese Communist Party recently celebrated its 100th anniversary, so the government in Beijing is very comfortable labelling itself 'communist'. Yes, they are deeply authoritarian, and while President Xi Jinping is now pursuing a stronger socialist course and wanting to fulfil the dreams of national destiny held by his parents' generation, who founded the PRC, the actual behaviour of people in China today is in general far more vibrantly capitalist than that of most Australians. The saying 'To get rich is glorious' is attributed to Deng Xiaoping, but even if he did not say these exact words, the sentiment certainly took hold across the country, with business and trade at every level becoming central to almost every relationship. This has produced a freewheeling 'cowboy capitalism' which I suspect is closer to the United States of the nineteenth century than either side would care to admit—'the Wild East', perhaps. In China, making money has come to have an almost moral power, and the aspirations of 1.4 billion people for a better life have been a truly formidable driving force for very rapid economic growth. Without the social constraints of a widely respected and independent legal system, however, China has accepted an authoritarian style of government to hold its vast society together.

President Xi recently changed the mantra to that of 'common prosperity', animated by the cutting down of multibillionaires, with the aim of raising the living standards of those on the lower rungs of Chinese society. Interestingly, China and the United States are both countries that exhibit gross inequalities of wealth and opportunity across their societies. And while we might not like the brutality and speed of the actions taken by the Chinese to address this issue, we can at least acknowledge that China is trying not to allow such inequalities to destroy its society in a comparable way to that which they observe is happening in the United States, where money, and the power that comes with it, corrupts the electoral and democratic processes. In Australia, the social democratic values of a progressive taxation system that redistributes income to, and provides services for, those with less, have taken something of a beating in recent years, but they are still meant to underlie our own form of government, which claims to promote the good of all, or, dare I say it, common prosperity. Only hardened ideologues believe that there can be no virtue, let alone good intention, in a society labelled 'communist'.

Most Australians of European heritage, and sadly most of the Australian political class, know almost nothing of China's history, its rich culture and traditions, let alone its language and government. Nor, it seems, do they see this as a weakness, because they certainly do not make any effort to learn about these things. In my lifetime, I don't think we have had a prime minister, a foreign minister, a deputy prime minister or even a wider Cabinet who have less knowledge of China, and less apparent interest in changing this dismal situation, than the incumbents at the time of writing. With a few exceptions, they are a deeply and depressingly mediocre lot. They haven't taken Asian history courses at school or university, and few have travelled to China or tried to forge real friendships with the people there. Contrast this with China, where members of the Politburo Standing Committee of the Chinese Communist Party (the very top leadership) are almost all, including Xi Jinping himself, said to speak English well, and many of them have studied overseas at some of the world's best universities.

Foreign Minister Wang Yi, for instance, attended graduate school at Georgetown University in Washington, DC and speaks both impeccable English and Japanese. In the Anglosphere, on the other hand, we are lazy and arrogant, believing it is everybody else's responsibility to learn our language while we don't have to make any effort to learn theirs. Language, of course, is central to an understanding of culture and ways of thinking. Our two languages and our mindsets work very differently, yet Australia insists on interpreting China only through a Western mindset which we believe to be the blueprint for wisdom and truth.

Despite their ignorance, our politicians and our media don't want to understand China. They want to change it. And now, as cheerleaders in the American rush towards greater conflict, they want us to dislike and fear China as well.

Outside of a small number of academics and, of course, the many Australians of Chinese descent now living here, the overwhelming majority of Australians know nothing of the suffering and trials of the Chinese people in the nineteenth and twentieth centuries, mostly inflicted by our British and European ancestors. They know little, and care less, about the rise of modern China and its legitimate interests, about the achievements of the Chinese people over the last few decades, during which hundreds of millions of people have been lifted out of poverty and enabled to live a modest but decent life—to have ownership of their own apartment, maybe also a car (and, because of sound government policies, increasingly it is likely to be an electric car), to take a holiday, in fact to enjoy a small share of the many privileges that Australians take for granted.

I have been travelling to China for over forty years and have only ever been met with, and tried to reciprocate, courtesy, curiosity and generosity. I can say very truthfully that, in general, the Chinese people are happier, more optimistic about the future, prouder of their own country, and more respectful of the value and power of a good education than the majority of Australians. Look at the old people dancing in the parks, or the fashion-conscious young in the major cities, or families enjoying a meal together at a restaurant—they look content with their lives, even if they are living modestly, and you get no sense at all that they feel oppressed by the heavy hand of the Communist Party, as some here want us to believe. Like most people around the world, the Chinese read about, and make jokes about, domestic politics, but to most, politics are thought to belong to another sphere—someone else's sphere entirely. What most people want is to be left alone to get on with their lives, to enjoy their families, do their jobs and make money. It was so in China's imperial past, and so it is today.

HITCHING THE NATIONAL WAGON, DITCHING OUR NATIONAL SOVEREIGNTY

In Australia over the last five years, the mainstream media commentary on China has become consistently and aggressively hostile. Why do so many of those who carry influence and weight in our society spout negative, ill-informed judgements about so many aspects of the bilateral relationship, not just in terms of great-power security or economic threat, but worse, in terms of some supposed irreconcilable conflict of objectives and common human concerns? Partly it is because senior members of our current government spout anti-Chinese sentiments all the time. Partly it is because much of the commentary about China is sourced from the United States where, since 2016 when Trump came to office, China has been seen as the enemy, a direct threat to American exceptionalism. It also reads to me as part of the same, continuing, deep insecurity that has bedevilled the Australian imagination since the arrival of the First Fleet: that we are a threatened and fearful white enclave alone in a teeming and inherently hostile Asian sea. Having stolen this land and been responsible for the deaths of the majority of its former inhabitants, I suppose colonial Australia had cause to feel insecure that the process might be repeated by the yellow hordes sweeping down from the north. We have therefore always needed and sought to find a big brother as our protector.

Some of our politicians may deny it, but there is also a strong stain of racism in the Australian make-up. A very large number of white Australians think themselves superior to other people of different skin colour. In our geographic context, after the mistreatment of Indigenous people, this is mostly directed at people of Asian descent. There is a long and unattractive history here.

The mid-nineteenth-century anti-Chinese riots and other violence on the colonial goldfields are well known. The imagined menace used to be characterised as the 'Yellow Peril'. Now, a pallid version of American ideological prejudice has been added to the racial poison. Reminiscent of Arthur Miller's play *The Crucible*, today it is sufficient just to add the word 'communist' to the racial kindling as the fire-starter.

Mixing elements of racism, ignorance and ideology, many Australians are also still trapped in a time warp, imagining the Chinese masses as poor and backward coolies, the 'workers, peasants and soldiers' of the Cultural Revolution years, toiling like ants in blue or khaki serge with shovels and pitchforks in hand: how is it possible that these people have created a modern industrial society so swiftly? Suddenly, some people find it very threatening that many Chinese are richer than us, more successful than us, and often smarter than us.

These Bolshie Chinese even presume to question the eternal truth of our Western so-called 'universal values'. Would these happen to be the same values exhibited by our British forebears who stole the land, massacred the Indigenous inhabitants, and more recently took the children away from their mothers in order to make them more like us? Or the values that keep children and families imprisoned year after year, without end, in detention centres on distant islands for the supposed 'crime' of wanting to escape the tyranny of war and give their children a basic chance in life? It is time we stopped feeling so self-righteous. Every society has strengths and weaknesses. We need to be a lot more clear-eyed about both and focus on addressing our own issues.

I suspect that the majority of Australians will have heard of the Great Wall of China, which was built over many hundreds of years through different dynasties. Following multiple courses and spanning over 20 000 kilometres, it was defensive in intention and planning, with regular watchtowers and troop barracks, built to keep out various invading groups, including the Mongols. Like the traditional courtyard houses in Beijing, or the walls you see around factories in the countryside, it was designed for protection, to keep people out. China looks inwards.

In the early fifteenth century, the Chinese explorer and admiral Zheng He led voyages to South-East Asia, the Indian subcontinent and

East Africa. He didn't plant flags or claim to have discovered these lands. Rather, he traded, explored and collected treasure. It was not much later that the Ming emperors became more concerned with the threat of Mongol invasion and largely disowned their own remarkable naval exploits. In 1793, the Qianlong Emperor was courteous in receiving the 1st Earl George Macartney's diplomatic mission to China, which had been sent by King George III, but he saw no need to allow the opening of new ports for the import of British manufactures, nor the establishment of a permanent embassy in Beijing. Traditionally, the Chinese have felt themselves to be self-sufficient.

Unlike the British and other European powers of the nineteenth century, and the United States of the twentieth century, China's history has not been one of international conquest and expansion. The Chinese diaspora is spread around the globe not as a result of China's imperial ambition and strength, but rather because of its weakness and poverty, which, for almost 200 years, until the second half of the twentieth century, forced people to seek better lives elsewhere. Australia has been the beneficiary of this, with around 1.3 million Chinese people now living here, although their talents and connections are sadly under-utilised.

Late in 2020, our Prime Minister was reported as saying words to the effect that 'The relationship with China is hard and it is going to get harder'. Why have I never heard him say, 'How are we going to try to make it better?' Sadly, I have not seen much evidence that he and his advisers want the relationship to get better. It's scary, but maybe he does not know how to make it better. Even scarier, perhaps he is waiting for instructions from Washington before he tries to make it better. But as in a failing marriage, things won't improve without the serious will to make this happen. Australia seems to have lost its independent resolve and agency.

Simply sitting it out, known in political speak as 'strategic patience', is not going to work, a least not in my lifetime. Frankly, China has largely ceased to care about Australia. Politically we have made ourselves irrelevant. Australia is seen as America's shoeshine boy in the South Pacific. John Howard described us as the 'Deputy Sheriff', a phrase that has stuck, while the Chinese invoke less-flattering labels meaning we are 'America's gofer' (to use the film industry term). Australia's relationship with

China certainly won't get better through bluster and slogans, such as our PM talking sternly of 'sovereignty', which is not at issue—the Chinese are not about to invade us—or of our 'values', which are not threatened—the Chinese are not asking us to change our form or government, follow Confucius, change our language or unpick our legal system.

Our sovereignty is indeed threatened, but not by an aggressive China. Rather, we ourselves have given it away to the United States, gradually since World War II, but more recently in a rush, with the Australia–United States Ministerial Consultations (AUSMIN) in Washington over the past decade, and the September 2021 AUKUS pact centred on a nuclear submarine deal. Should the aforementioned submarines ever arrive—the first one is not due until 2040, despite the defence minister's claim that a Chinese threat is imminent—the Australian Navy will be subsumed (submerged?) into the US chain of command. The Prime Minister assured us that the nuclear reactors would simply be dropped into hulls to be built in Adelaide, and we wouldn't need to raise a spanner for the thirty-plus-years' life of the vessels. Pull the other one. Australia can't even keep six diesel subs in workable condition. If we are not allowed to understand the technology and we cannot service our own vessels, in what sense can we say that we control our own armed forces? If we have yielded their control to the United States in the name of 'interoperability', we really have become a mere pawn in America's games—and the tragedy for Australia is that the game they favour is the war game.

Already there are US bases on Australian soil over which we have no control. Pine Gap, the surveillance base near Alice Springs in the Northern Territory, would immediately be targeted if the United States became entangled in a war with China because it is understood to be an integral part of the US war machine, communicating with American satellites and submarines around the globe. We are already complicit in the use of Pine Gap in the Central Intelligence Agency's illegal drone assassination program in the Middle East and South Asia. Next, we will have American nuclear-armed ships home-porting in Australia under the AUSMIN agreement, offering 'combined logistics, sustainment and maintenance enterprise to support high end warfighting and combined military operations in the region'. Virtually without public discussion, let alone open parliamentary debate, Australia has thrown away its sovereignty and become a major US military base for a possible war against China. Is that in our own national interest? Is it a price worth paying just because the Coalition government thinks it will help them win elections? How can our political leaders display so little wisdom? Do we as Australians really want to make ourselves and our major cities prime targets in such a war?

With AUKUS, we hitched the national wagon to two declining powers: the United States, an immensely powerful but practically failing democracy, and the United Kingdom, which lost its empire long ago and really has no business in the Pacific. The United Kingdom's last war with China was conducted in order to force the latter to accept shiploads of opium at a time when this drug was even banned on UK soil. The British have further antagonised Europe, which plays to the strategic advantage of China (and even more to that of Russia), through the weakening of the US–Europe alliance. For Australia to be clinging to an Anglophone partnership when we live in a multilingual Asian world also damages perceptions of us in our region, except perhaps with Japan, where the longstanding White Australia policy long ago entrenched our image as a racist, white colonial outpost. The OKKERS alliance only confirms the stereotype that some have fought long and hard to change.

The Prime Minister says that every decision he makes on China is 'in the national interest'. I find it difficult to understand how decisions that concede our ability to act independently, while at the same time severely alienating our biggest trading partner and damaging export earnings, can possibly be in Australia's national interest. The 'trade war' with China actually serves the interests of the United States, which has taken our place as a seller of the barley used to make Chinese beer, and replaced Western Australian crayfish with Boston lobster in upmarket Chinese restaurants. And we may have lost a free-trade agreement with Europe because of our appalling treatment of France over the termination of their submarine contract—cancelling a $90 billion contract by text message has to be a Personal Best, if not an Olympic record! But we have certainly helped the French wine industry, and indeed that of our mates in New Zealand, both of whose vintages now replace Australia's on the shelves of Chinese bottle shops.

SHIFTING THE CENTRE OF GRAVITY

Why is it, do you think, that the many different countries of the Asian region are able to deal with China so much better than we do, even the ones which have favoured an alliance with America and/or have a troubled history with China itself? Japan has huge historical baggage to contend with in its dealings with China, and the two nations are so close geographically that they continue to argue fiercely over an uninhabited rocky outcrop in their shared sea, yet the Japanese seem to manage the relationship so much better than Australia. Courtesy, discipline, respect and an intimate knowledge of the other are a good start, but these are not the values you associate with our management of the relationship with China. Another factor is a more independent foreign policy. The Japanese have deep concerns about the growth of China; they favour America; they are members of the Quad, whose primary reason for existence is the containment of China. But, unlike Australia, the Japanese are not willing to jump every time America tells them to—and, of course, they know how to decline such requests with infinite politeness. The Japanese understand that their national interest is not identical to America's, let alone Australia's.

Despite occasional outbreaks of community violence against its own citizens of Chinese heritage, one of our nearest neighbours, Indonesia, with whom Australia also should be much more closely allied, still manages to walk the line between China and America with so much more subtlety and finesse than we can. If you look at a map, it is obvious that if Australia were really concerned about the threat posed by China, we would make every possible effort to be as friendly as possible with Indonesia, whose 6000 islands and 275 million people offer a natural security umbrella for us. Yet now we have surprised and offended Indonesia once again with the AUKUS announcement, although they have been very polite in public with their talk of concern about nuclear proliferation. Like Indonesia, the city-state of Singapore, and for that matter New Zealand, whom we think of as close family, also manage to negotiate their relationships with China with vastly more tact than we can muster.

None of these countries spend as much time and political capital as we do needlessly poking China in the eye, and none have had their trade with China threatened as we have. They treat China with public and formal diplomatic respect, as one should treat one's neighbours, particularly the very big and powerful ones with whom you want strong commercial relations.

Our relationship with China went into freefall when Prime Minister Morrison chose to attach himself at the hip to a US president who not only did not drain the swamp, he *was* the swamp—a president who went out of his way to destroy the international organisations and norms that we constantly say we want others to support; a president who belittled the alliances on which our security was said to depend, and who humiliated the leaders of friendly democratic countries while praising and protecting autocrats. I don't know what flattery spiked our Prime Minister's drink at the state dinner Trump hosted at the White House in September 2019, but, like another political intern, he was clearly seduced. Perhaps it could be said metaphorically that he sold our national soul for the dinner's Dover sole. For afters, Trump served the PM a high US military honour, the Legion of Merit. Save us! When I think of the cost, I suspect this is possibly Australia's most expensive meal ever.

Perhaps I should not be so hard on our PM. After all, he has been acting in that great Australian tradition of subservience—some would even call it loyalty—first directed at the British motherland, and then, after World War II, at our new big brother, the United States. A century ago, this loyalty took us into World War I, and especially into Gallipoli, where the first lord of the British Admiralty, Winston Churchill, determined that Australian diggers should take on the Turks in the hills fronting the Dardanelles. Both sides suffered appalling casualties, but the Turks won the battle while Australia licked its wounds and mythologised its loss.

After Word War II, Australia's loyalties switched from Great Britain to the United States, and despite widespread protests, our government under prime minister Harold Holt decided to go 'All the way with LBJ' in support of America's mistaken war in Vietnam. That support came at a very high cost: 521 Australian soldiers died in the Vietnam War, including 200 conscripts, and over 3000 were wounded. The conflict scarred a divided nation.

In another bout of insecurity and a holding aloft of the ANZUS treaty, in the wake of the 9/11 attacks on New York and Washington, at the request of the Americans, Australia sent troops to fight in Afghanistan. The fact that the 9/11 perpetrators were Saudis and not Afghans did not worry our government, nor did the fact that they were unable to define clearly our mission—was it to fight al-Qaeda, support the Afghan people in finding prosperity, bring democracy to people who hadn't asked for it, or train Afghan troops? Over the duration of this interminable war, there was so much changing of objectives that it could only end badly. It did, and again our subservience came at a very high cost. Despite the many subsequent political homilies, most Australians are wise enough to know we should not have been on the other side of the world participating in another US-led failure.

In 2003, when we joined US and British forces in invading Iraq, the official mission was to locate and destroy suspected weapons of mass destruction. Such weapons were never found, but Australian forces in various modest configurations were bogged down for eight years in yet another destructive war. The chaos in the Middle East that resulted from this conflict has caused many hundreds of thousands of civilian casualties and cost billions of Australian taxpayer dollars. It also led to a protracted Australian military presence in that part of the world, and has left the region more unstable and dangerous than before. How is that in our national interest?

> As flies to wanton boys, are we to the gods;
> They kill us for their sport
>> *King Lear*, Act 4 Scene 1

All these wars have revealed Australia to be a loyal ally that jumps when America tells us to, but none of them have made us safer. Nor have they made America safer, nor its leadership more widely admired. We have always been told that Australia will not have to choose between its history and its geography, but our Prime Minister has chosen for us (or was it really Peter Dutton?) and once again the Americans are leading us towards confrontation, perhaps even war, this time with China. The United States always exaggerates the dangers posed by its supposed enemies, and now it is consciously working itself up into a lather about China. It is working Australia up, too. First it was trade, then it was the threat to our sovereignty, now it's Taiwan. Isn't it time to develop a more independent foreign policy that retains the United States as a friend but also develops a more balanced, diplomatic and nuanced relationship with China? Contrary to the defence doomsayers and media pundits, we do not have to sell our soul to achieve this. Europe hasn't. New Zealand hasn't. Indonesia hasn't. Singapore hasn't.

Trump said he was going to 'Make America Great Again'. Only one wrong word here. In fact, Trump did more than anyone else to 'Make *China* Great Again'. No wonder they wanted to see him re-elected. China has been on a trajectory leading back to historical greatness since Deng Xiaoping kickstarted economic reforms in the countryside of Sichuan Province in the late 1970s, but the sheer incompetence and corruption of the Trump administration proved to be a massive free kick and contributed enormously to speeding the shift in the world's centre of gravity from the Atlantic to the Asia-Pacific. China is now the major regional player in the Asia-Pacific, although the development of India and of various members of the Association of Southeast Asian Nations has also contributed to the overall rebalancing. The economic crisis of 2008–09, which started on Wall Street and did so much damage across the Western world, also influenced this relatively rapid reframing of power. Another major factor, of course, has been the single-minded and long-sighted push by Xi Jinping and his government to rebuild China's pre-eminence in regional strategic and military strength. President Xi feels that China's time as a superpower is here, and the majority of the Chinese population are immensely proud this is so—they, too, believe their time has come.

Until quite recently, our politicians regularly reassured us that the global balance of power would remain in America's favour through most of the twenty-first century. They don't say that now, not when most respectable economists (if that is not an oxymoron!) predict that China's growth means that it will surpass the United States in economic terms around 2030. And not when the military balance is becoming more even, with China rapidly building the capacity to defend itself and challenge American naval superiority in the Western Pacific.

WHAT CHINA REALLY WANTS

It is very important that Australia asks itself what China really wants. I think that, first, it is to be the undisputed leading power in the Western Pacific, or East Asia, or the Indo-Pacific as some have taken to calling it, as though this very name somehow reduces China's influence. Second, China wants to be respected as a superpower equal to the United States in its broad influence in world affairs. I would argue that, in view of its giant landmass and population, its economic strength, developed infrastructure and military capacity, the first goal is not objectively unreasonable, but it does require the United States—and Australia too—to accept China's rise rather than attempt so strenuously to contain it; America should understand the logic and desirability of being the dominant player in your own backyard, just as they are in Latin America and the Caribbean. The second objective will take a bit longer, but in principle a balance of power is not a bad thing.

The Chinese regard what we call 'the South China Sea' as their own backyard. Their economy depends massively on the export of manufactured goods, and they know there are several chokepoints where this sea trade could be denied, especially by submarine blockade. That is why they see control of this space as so important for their own economic, and thus political, survival. From the Chinese perspective, this is a defensive strategy—their new Great Wall. Yes, as the US media constantly tell us, it means that China is acting in violation of international law, but what the Americans fail to remind us is that they themselves have never agreed to ratify the UN Convention on the Law of the Sea, so their objection is without strong grounds. All superpowers behave badly, but the Americans seem desperately to want to retain this right for themselves. Instead of sending weaponised armadas to claim 'freedom of navigation' in a provocative act of muscle flexing, wouldn't diplomacy and direct negotiations led by the regional countries most closely involved—Vietnam, the Philippines, Malaysia and Brunei—be a better solution? Why doesn't Australia support this? Try to imagine the American response if the Chinese were to send battleships into the Gulf of Mexico in the name of 'freedom of navigation'.

Knowing very little himself, and without a mind of his own except when it comes to his own re-election, our Prime Minister has unfortunately chosen to take his advice on China, and content for his speeches about China, from a very small group of people in the defence and intelligence world, all trained by and taking their cues from the US defence and intelligence establishment in Washington, and all actively hostile to China. For now, they show no sign of recognising that the realities on the ground have changed, nor, like their American mentors, that they want the Sino-Australian relationship to improve.

What we seem not to understand is China's demand for 'respect' as a necessary basis for reciprocal and productive cooperation. This means accepting the People's Republic of China for what it is: a state in the international system as legitimate as any other, with its own system of government and its own power structures. This is the state with which Australia established diplomatic relations in 1972 when our government signed up unambiguously to the 'One China' policy, which does not recognise

Taiwan (or 'the Republic of China', as the island calls itself) as a sovereign nation but rather as part of the PRC. It is the same state with which we developed a close and most productive bilateral relationship over forty years. China has been a communist state throughout this period, but for a long time this was not an ideological impediment to mutual respect and mutually beneficial cooperation. Today, however, as the Chinese have made abundantly clear, a lack of respect is the core political problem at the heart of our relationship.

'Respect' is clearly not part of the vocabulary of those now running the China relationship in Australia, the defence and intelligence folk who rather are paid to see threats, to look into the future to divine the shape of wars to come. Their currency, borrowed from the Americans, is to give credibility and respectability to fear. They pump out press releases and give favoured journalists background briefings; they write speeches for our leaders about China's challenge to our independence and the loss of Australian sovereignty.

There are two problems with this. First, defence people tend to be lousy analysts of historical trends, let alone of what is happening now. Look at recent history, in particular the staggering cost blowouts and disastrous problems and switches with our proposed submarine fleet and the Joint Strike Fighter program. Second, it is simply wrong to say that China is a threat to Australian sovereignty. Yes, the Chinese are throwing their weight around and they sometimes behave belligerently, but we should be used to that—it is what great powers do, as the Americans have always illustrated. We are not told that the United States has around 800 military bases around the world, while China has only one outside its own territory, in Djibouti. We are not reminded that the United States has drawn us into several wars that were clearly not in our national interest to help wage, unless sold through the lens of paying insurance, which of course no Australian government dare confess. Unlike the United States, China doesn't want to station its troops and military hardware here, nor is it about to invade, but it is unquestionably on its way to achieving the status of a superpower, as it was 200 years ago. After a century or so as the big boy on the block, the Americans simply don't like this, so they tell us not to like it, and our government says, 'Yes sir, no sir, three bags full, sir.'

Of course, the analysis of strategic threats is a very important element in any assessment of our national security, and the government must hear this voice, but it can become a self-fulfilling threat when it is the *only* voice that is heard. Since when has Australia's economic security not been a critical part of our national security? Since when is it OK to destroy Australian jobs and livelihoods by locking our position in with that of the blinkered view of American exceptionalism that allows no competitor to even enter the field, let alone challenge the status quo? Have our political leaders worked out where they are leading us if we continue down this same path?

Why isn't our government listening to views on the China relationship from leaders in Australian business, science and technology, education, diplomacy, arts and culture, minerals and energy, law, indeed the large universe of those involved in the widest range of commercial, cultural and people-to-people engagement with China? Only five very short years ago, such people were considered important contributors to Australia's wide-ranging and successful relationship. It is true that China has become more and more assertive in its stance, but we must learn to deal with this as others do. Instead, we have gone out of our way to antagonise the Chinese and done almost nothing to understand their view of the world. The federal government even attacks the academic freedom of our own scholars who try to put forward more nuanced and independent views. Look at their flagrant defunding and removal of tax-deductible gift recipient status of the independent think tank China Matters in an attempt to silence them. Australian universities have been required to submit their faculty and PhD students to outrageous examinations of their loyalty. At some universities, academics who study China are even being censored by their administrators, who fear further funding cuts. Instead of seeking to undermine scholarship and our fine universities in these ongoing 'culture wars', why isn't our national government actively promoting serious study of China and investing in language training so that the next generation might be able to handle these things better?

Even some very senior Australian figures, including former politicians, have not escaped the expanding anti-communist dragnet. Former foreign minister Gareth Evans at least had the standing and the wit to laugh out of court the request from the Attorney-General's Department to register as a potential agent of foreign influence under new national security laws. I find it ironic that this Australian behaviour should prompt echoes of China's Cultural Revolution, when it was unsafe to have views outside the government-approved orthodoxy.

I used to jest that Xi Jinping and Donald Trump went to the same academy but fell out when Trump the narcissist threw a tantrum because he wanted to have what Xi has—no term limit as commander in chief, acknowledgement and praise heaped on him as chairman of and authority on everything, the ability to exercise total autocratic control. As US president, Trump would have loved to think of himself, and have others think of him, as the 'core navigator and helmsman'. I also used to jest—though it is not at all funny—that Rupert Murdoch is so virulently anti-China because he is letting off steam about his failed marriage with Wendy Deng and because his business interests were blocked there.

There is lots to criticise about China, as there is about practically every country on the planet, including our own, but currently, if anyone dares to say anything positive about China, Australian Government ministers slap them down no matter how senior or expert they may be. They are called 'Panda Huggers' or labelled in the Murdoch press as threats to our way of life. We are warned that the Chinese seek world domination and that we should be cutting them out and cutting them down, treating them as enemies. Is that really the best approach?

I myself was named among the Panda Huggers in Clive Hamilton's book *Silent Invasion* because I promoted one of the great ballet companies of the world, the National Ballet Company of China, in the program of the first Triennial of Asian Performing Arts (or 'Asia TOPA', as it is known) at Arts Centre Melbourne in 2017. Two years later, I gave a lecture at Western Sydney University which I titled 'Hugging Bears', the theme of which was that it was possible to be a deeply patriotic and loyal Australian working for our country's good, as I am, and simultaneously to love the high-quality expressions of another culture—or, as I framed it, to hug both koalas and pandas at the same time.

While we have been encouraged to think of every Chinese student as a potential spy, every business deal with China as a threat to national security, every example of research cooperation as selling out to the Chinese military and giving advantage to the communists, Australians of Chinese heritage, some of whose families have been here for six or more generations, are experiencing increasing racism and even physical threats. They are reluctant to participate in Australian civil society lest they be tarred with claims of disloyalty. Government inaction in response to this suggests that these Australians are seen as mere 'collateral damage', or perhaps that the situation is even a positive if it scares off a potent source of criticism of the government's stance against China. If you watch commercial TV stations or read the Murdoch press, you will notice that only Chinese Australians with anti-China views are acceptable to these media outlets, while those who might express support are too scared to speak, and yet we claim to be a country that celebrates freedom of speech.

In an October 2020 Senate committee hearing on diversity, Liberal Party Senator Eric Abetz demanded that several Australian Chinese

condemn 'the Chinese Communist Party dictator-
ship', a McCarthyist act of racial profiling to impose
a loyalty test based on one's ethnicity. Imagine the
media outcry if a Chinese Government committee
grilling Chinese Australians in Beijing demanded
that they condemn Australia's conservative government because of its human rights abuses
against asylum seekers and Indigenous people.
No wonder Australian Chinese are significantly
under-represented in positions of leadership across
society, as Gareth Evans illustrated in his 2019 Sir
Edward 'Weary' Dunlop Asialink lecture on breaking through 'the bamboo ceiling' in this country.
I know Australian Chinese who are now reluctant to
make donations to worthy charitable causes, even
to the arts, lest they be accused by our media of
trying to buy influence in Australian society.

CLINGING TO POWER

The Australian political class, which is predomi-
nantly Anglo, white and male, has been persuaded
to adopt increasingly hostile positions regarding
China in every field. And I am not just talking
about the conservatives—the Labor Party fears

being wedged and its members, with the occasional exception of Senator Penny Wong, are shamefully reluctant to express more balanced views lest they be branded as soft on national security. In an important speech she made in May 2021 to launch journalist Peter Hartcher's book *Red Zone*, Senator Wong made the point that everything said about China and every action taken towards China by the Prime Minister was done with an eye to his domestic political advantage. I believe this is correct, but only partly so. While it is true that focus groups may have been telling the Prime Minister that there are votes in claiming to stand up to China, I speculate that what has actually been happening is a proxy fight between the PM and challenger Peter Dutton for the leadership of the Coalition. Every time Dutton appeals to the far right by attacking China, the Prime Minister feels he has to say something even stronger to keep the right wings of both the Liberals and the Nationals on his team. He has the very slimmest of majorities in both his party and the parliament—he loses both if Dutton siphons off any of this support.

The party political motives behind the timing of the AUKUS alliance and the nuclear submarine announcement also seemed blatantly obvious. The federal government was on the nose for its monumental failure to purchase and distribute COVID-19 vaccines, thereby losing the advantage of Australia's early success in 2020 in containing the virus, and for failing to develop a proper national quarantine system to replace the state-based use of city hotels not designed for that purpose. The submarine deal was seen both as a good news distraction to take the electorate's collective mind off the government's poor management of the pandemic, and as a khaki election vote winner. Once again, the spineless ALP Opposition lent its support because it did not want to be characterised as weak on national security.

Why do I think the AUKUS/submarines announcement was part of an election strategy? Because, while you might make a strong case for the merits of nuclear submarines as part of the national defence strategy, why was this case not made a few years earlier before the signing of the contract with France for diesel submarines? My belief was strengthened by the fact that the announcement made no mention of the cost—both financial and in terms of our national reputation—of breaking the contract for the French-designed submarines.

Australia reportedly spent $2.5 billion before doing so and now faces a bill for many more billions. And with France, at the time of writing about to assume the presidency of the European Union, it also appeared set to cost Australia its coveted free-trade agreement with the EU, a loss that is hardly in our national interest. People forget that France is a significant player in the Pacific and had seen the relationship with Australia sealed with Morrison's bonhomie as both welcoming and reinforcing its role as an international power. The recall of the French ambassador and France's bitter language of betrayal, treason and lies in late 2021 clearly indicated Australia's careless diplomatic naivety.

Interestingly, the submarine announcement also made no mention of the cost of the eight nuclear vessels, except that it would be more than the $90 billion that was going to be charged for the twelve cancelled French subs—the issue of cost was left to be pondered over subsequent months—nor whether we would be getting a US or UK model. Can you imagine a government decision in any other area of national life that involved a cost of at least $100 billion that was not accompanied by vastly more detail and planning? The government's annual budget for the arts, which might buy a pop-up toaster in one of the projected submarines, faces vastly more analysis and challenges from the government, Opposition and media.

As it turned out, the government got the blanket media attention it wanted, whereas analysis of the announcement over subsequent weeks dribbled out with far less notice. The fact that the first new submarine would not be available until after 2040 made nonsense of the government's claim that China was an imminent threat and, in any case, by that time the seas will likely be dominated by unmanned underwater drones. The idea that Adelaide could build such technologically sophisticated vessels was also laughed out of court, but don't worry about the little things when the media moment has been won.

Similarly searching for more evidence of communist cunning and more media moments celebrating our country's heroic stance, in 2020 the government said it needed to review every sister-state and sister-city relationship with China, and every linkage and research partnership between Australian universities and their Chinese counterparts. Special legislation was brought in to legitimise this, but we were told—wink wink—that

this was not just about China but about our relations with every country. If so, the parliamentary
committee established to look at such relations is
going to be very busy indeed. I've been told that
across the wide operations of Melbourne University
alone, there are over 4000 partnership agreements
with other universities and research institutes
around the world. Nationally, there will be tens of
thousands of international cooperation agreements
among Australian universities but, let me guess, the
committee will only look at those agreements that
involve China—though perhaps Iran and North
Korea too, just to show how even-handed we are!

Let me guess again: the committee will not look
at our sister-state and sister-city relations with
Japan and other countries around the world, but it
will pore over those with China, such as Victoria–
Jiangsu and Melbourne–Tianjin. None of these have
yet been cancelled, but they remain under threat
until such time as the federal government says this
is off the table. How innocent we were. We thought
that these relationships, many of them introduced
with positive fanfare by conservative state and city
governments, were a wonderful bridge for mutually
beneficial exchanges in culture, sport, education,

and social and economic development, when really they were insidious instruments of strategic threat from those cunning communists!

The federal government believes state politicians, and particularly Labor premiers, simply don't read the tea leaves or understand the dangers. In 2020, Victorian premier Dan Andrews became a target for having sought to enhance the state's economy and support wider employment through linkages with China. Only a few years beforehand, Andrews had been praised by the then federal Liberal government for his initiative in giving motherhood recognition to China's Belt and Road Initiative (BRI)—even our ambassador in Beijing had hosted a function to mark the occasion. Now, just a few years later, he was being vilified by Canberra. In April 2021, the Victorian agreement was cancelled on the grounds that the BRI was just a communist debt trap for unwary countries. What advantage did we achieve by cancelling an agreement under which no major Chinese investment in Victoria had been made, let alone any debt incurred? None. What other countries did we save from debt? None. All that the cancellation achieved was to provoke another negative Chinese response.

Clearly, that was the intention of this miserable gesture, one more suitable for the schoolyard than the realm of respectful international diplomacy.

In June 2020, a sitting NSW Labor MP, Shaoquett Moselmane, as part of a joint investigation with the Australian Security Intelligence Organisation (ASIO), had his home raided by the Federal Police, who were searching for evidence to support allegations of a Chinese Government plot to influence serving politicians. In an outrageous misuse of power, the raid was conducted in full view of the media, who had clearly been tipped off by ASIO or the Federal Police to maximise the political mileage in demonstrating tough government action. Unfortunately for the government, apparently no evidence was found, as no charges of any kind whatsoever followed, but no doubt the raids were considered successful because of the anti-Chinese media coverage they generated.

At the time of writing, the federal government was even looking at breaking the 99-year lease signed in 2015 with Landbridge, a Chinese enterprise, governing the operation of the Port of Darwin. This contract was willingly signed by a Liberal Northern Territory government with the blessing of a Liberal federal government. As part of normal commercial investment, Chinese corporations also hold different interests in the operations of the Port of Newcastle and the Port of Melbourne. If, at the urging of the United States, we now break any or all of these contracts, which were entered into in good faith, and with the Australian Government's blessing, it will not just prompt another negative Chinese reaction but further damage our international reputation and raise the so-called 'sovereign risk' of investing in Australia, dampening future economic prospects.

THE COST OF THE
FOREIGN INTERFERENCE BILL

In the government's own press release about the China–Australia Free Trade Agreement (ChAFTA), which came into force in December 2015, the arrangement was described as 'an historic Agreement that is delivering enormous benefits to Australia, enhancing our competitive position in the Chinese market, boosting economic growth and creating jobs'.[1] Just a few years later, we can see many examples of Australia's economic interest being swamped by Canberra's political posturing.

One example: in late 2020, Mengniu, a Chinese dairy company based in Inner Mongolia, was blocked from purchasing the Australia-based dairy and drinks business owned by Lion, a Japanese company. So: a publicly listed Chinese company had wanted to buy some Australian dairy assets from a publicly listed Japanese company in what had been approved as a straightforward $600 million commercial deal by Australia's own Foreign Investment Review Board. Treasurer Josh Frydenberg, however, personally made the call to stop the deal 'on national security grounds', or so he said. In fact, I think it had much more to do with the Canberra leadership waltz, with Frydenberg pushing back against Peter Dutton's leadership aspirations by showing off his own hairy-chested right-wing credentials. I imagine that in the Liberal party room, the decision was also thought to be appealing to the electorate, who have increasingly been encouraged to view anything Chinese as a negative.

What a pity Australia breached the terms of the ChAFTA by blocking this investment in what was considered to be a non-sensitive sector (sensitive sectors being defined to include media, telecommunications and defence-related industries). Who knew that the Chinese buying Japanese-owned dairy cows represented a national security threat? Who, like me, naively thought that the Australian Government supported a market economy, private business and a rules-based international trading order?

As China seeks to build its international clout, there is much irony in Western countries, especially the United States, with its political and economic weight, seeking to inhibit Chinese corporations. American trade restrictions have certainly damaged some major private Chinese companies as well as raised the costs of many goods in the US market. However, Chinese authorities tend to step in to support these companies, which gives the government an even stronger position in the national economy and simultaneously weakens the private sector, which has been the largest engine of Chinese growth in recent decades. As we have seen with the treatment of tech companies such as Alibaba, DiDi and Tencent, where the government wants them to serve the state through 'common prosperity', and not just the founders and financial investors, President Xi ends up smiling because one of his goals is to exert increased state control over all non-government players in the country's economic, social and cultural spheres.

Another consequence of this anti-China stance is that it is encouraging the Chinese to build 'a parallel universe in trade, technology and finance that will selectively reduce its vulnerabilities to American hegemony'. The BRI, which President Xi has made his own big foreign policy push, is 'creating a Sino-centric system of specifications, standards, norms and regulations that will favour China's technology and services to the exclusion of others'.[2] In this sense, 'One Belt, One Road', or 'the New Silk Road', as it is sometimes called, is a Chinese push to extend influence particularly, but not only, across the vast landmass of Central Asia towards the Mediterranean, where once traders and adventurers braved vast deserts and high mountain passes on the ancient Silk Road.

The West's recent and precipitous defeat in Afghanistan will mean increased Chinese investment in that country, which is strategically positioned along the Silk Road. The new Taliban leadership quickly met with the Chinese foreign minister and other Beijing officials. It seems that, in return for the Taliban holding back support for any Uyghur separatist movement in Xinjiang, China has agreed to make substantial investments in Afghanistan. Western governments do not like it, but China is almost always prepared to do business with other countries without seeking to change the nature of the recipient government, including imposing on them their own model of human rights. I would predict that, within a relatively short span of years, Chinese fast-train routes across Central Asia will run through Kabul. That is surely a good thing if you believe that opening up an isolated 'closed' country will introduce new ideas and economic modernisation.

While China may have taken the investment lustre off some of their giant technology companies and, in all likelihood, gained access to those organisations' vast stores of data, they still want the companies to be very successful. Learning from America, the Chinese Government understands the enormous amount of influence and control that can stem from national and international digital platforms in particular. Extending the influence of their own technology platforms is, of course, exactly what the Americans did in the late twentieth century—think Facebook, Google and Amazon. By banning these platforms in China, the government actually created space for their own indigenous platforms to develop and prosper in the huge domestic market. Notwithstanding the wailing of the foreign financial press, I do not believe that the Chinese want to destroy some of their most successful companies ever, but they do want them to serve the national interest. The Western media have attacked China for seeking to reign in what the Chinese see as the negative influences of powerful high-tech platforms, but at the same time, the United States, Europe and Australia are each seeking to legislate to bring these under tighter control and to stamp out some of their negative social impacts.

More than any security threat, I am inclined to think that the American push to cut back Chinese leadership in 5G was the primary reason they wanted Australia, the United Kingdom and other nations to ban Huawei technology from their 5G networks. It is ironic, then, to see that China is now emboldened to go its own way and develop its own internationally powerful brands that could soon dominate large parts of the world, including South-East Asia, Central Asia and Africa.

Our government constantly tells us that foreign interference is a huge threat, but it is obvious that we are not really against foreign interference, just against what Australia sees as Chinese interference. We don't ban other nations from promoting their interests here—indeed we welcome it, sometimes even celebrate it. We don't hassle the Japan Foundation or the Goethe Institute for teaching Japanese or German and promoting their national cultures to Australians. And despite the passage through federal parliament in September 2019 of the Foreign Relations (State and Territory) Arrangements Bill, known in shorthand as the Foreign Interference Bill, which was pressed on the government by our national security agencies, we have American military bases on our land with US troops, and long-range-bomber training based near Darwin. This military presence is now going to expand many times over under AUSMIN agreements and the AUKUS alliance. Isn't this foreign interference, and something that is much more likely to drag us into a future war than keep us out?

Another example: an American citizen controls a large percentage of the Australian media landscape, and year after year he uses his power and influence to undermine public broadcasting and exert direct and extremely overt influence on federal election outcomes. Isn't it foreign interference when even the most conservative Australian prime ministers have to tithe and pay homage if they don't wish to be under daily assault on the front pages of the national and state-based papers in the Murdoch stable and on Sky News?

I do not wish to cause offence by this comment, but I would point out that foreign interference is actually written into our Constitution. Australia's head of state is a foreigner and, as was shown in 2020 with the release of formerly classified materials from the National Archives, Her Britannic Majesty is able to exert direct influence through Her staff and representatives concerning the dismissal of a democratically elected Australian head of government. Queen Elizabeth is a truly wonderful monarch for the United Kingdom but, at least for me, it is absurd, indeed almost obscene, that we are still subject to Her high-level foreign interference. Are we really still mentally imprisoned in a forelock-tugging convict and colonial past? It is time we grew up and practised exercising a more independent frame of mind.

SEEING THINGS DIFFERENTLY

Australia is in a very serious pickle strategically and economically. We fell into this situation very quickly—the downhill slide has only taken five years—by following a faltering star. This is costing us many tens of billions of dollars in lost export earnings and many Australian jobs every year. For some time, this real financial loss has been hidden by the high price paid by China for Australia's iron ore, while the decline in jobs and the wider social costs have been masked by the COVID-19 pandemic. Now China is cutting back both on steel production and demand for the alloy, especially in the housing sector, so the price of iron ore is dropping dramatically. When massive Chinese investment in alternative sources of iron ore come online in a few years, the bleeding obvious will become much more bloody and painful—unless we take action now. And, as Robert Gottliebsen pointed out in *The Australian* in the first half of 2021, we would be wise to remember that China controls a high percentage of all shipping that comes to this country.[3] Turn off this tap and Australian exports *and* imports will be severely compromised. Such actions might hurt the Chinese too, but don't count on them not being willing to pay the price.

We have been mired in this situation by a government that doesn't know how to get us out; indeed, a government that seemingly does not want to get us out. President Biden seems to have been talking to President Xi. Although US domestic politics are opposed to it, and the auguries don't look good, especially around the issue of Taiwan, the Biden Administration might find a pathway to improved US relations with China. Then, either Australia might follow, or perhaps we will be hung out to dry. Regardless, why must we wait for permission to act in our own national interest?

It wasn't always thus.

I was very lucky. My chance to deal with and work in China came in a period when Australia was beginning to see the opportunities that a modernising China represented for trade, when there was huge optimism that China's 'Open Door Policy' would not only offer commercial benefits through trade liberalisation but also, so it was thought, gradually nudge the country towards a more relaxed and accountable, if not democratic, system of government. We forgot that China had been run by imperial dynasties for thousands of years and that, despite the new communist branding, it was not about to change its fundamental form of government administration just because Australia and others in the West thought this was desirable. As a good friend said so memorably in another context altogether, 'You can't make a tree grow by shouting at it.'

It is worth stating clearly that most Chinese do not want the kind of democracy that we think would be good for them. That is simply not part of their DNA. They speak about themselves as a socialist democracy, but there is nothing in their education system that leads them to aspire towards democracy according to our terms. They see democracy as it is practised in the West as leading to chaotic and dysfunctional societies, not least in the United States, which captures enormous media space in China. They see and don't understand the political shambles of a contested US election in 2020 leading so far as an assault on Congress. They see and don't wish to emulate the focus on individual rights at the expense of the collective good. They read and don't comprehend how a country that claims to be a model democracy can have tens of millions of high-powered assault rifles circulating among its citizens, often carried openly, with stories of Chinese students being shot given media prominence. They see and don't like images of US racism and poverty.

I recall that when I was a kid, to prompt me to eat my dinner, I was told to remember the starving children of China. Chinese children, meanwhile, were told about the starving black children in America, where the dogs of the rich were better fed. Both stories had a significant element of truth. The point is that, from a distance, the other society does not look very attractive. We can't change this by wishing it away.

Of course, the Chinese media does not focus on what we perceive the theoretical merits of our democracy to be: the opportunity to choose our leaders; the ability to criticise those leaders vigorously; the right of appeal to an independent judiciary whose judgments are not based on political considerations; the subservience of the defence forces to the civilian government. In my observation, however, the vast majority of Chinese people do not believe they are missing much. With some notable exceptions, by and large they do not share the Western view of human rights, but rather define these in more fundamental terms as the right to be lifted out of poverty, to be fed and housed. And they are happy to trade the opportunity to participate in politics for the freedom to pursue their own lives—to make money, raise their families, feel secure. They do not feel oppressed by the state. Our political leaders never try to imagine, let alone understand, what Chinese people might actually be thinking—they are far too busy telling us what they believe is wrong with Chinese thinking and lecturing the Chinese on how they should be thinking.

The China I worked within in the mid-1980s has long since gone. The country is vast and complex, changing so rapidly that it is not possible for anyone, much less a part-time observer like me, to keep pace. To help you understand what a different world it was back then, at that time emails were not yet used for daily communication, let alone the Chinese messaging platform WeChat. Amazon, Google, Facebook, Twitter, and the Chinese platforms Alibaba, Tencent and Baidu, did not yet exist.

My wife grew up during the Cultural Revolution and, coming from an artistic and intellectual family—'the ninth stinking class', as they were called in the rather colourful language of the time—they suffered a great deal. Her grandfather was killed in front of her, her parents were sent to a labour camp, her school was closed, and she was sent to live with relations on a naval base. She and others endured a decade of national chaos, personal tragedy, political isolation and economic disaster. Indeed, much of the nineteenth and twentieth centuries was marked by frequent chaos and war in China, often coming down on the nation from abroad. No wonder stability and order are such deeply held desires of ordinary Chinese people, not just values imposed from above. President Xi may be disliked and feared by the political and financial elites in China, but he is immensely popular among the common people because he represents stability and prosperity.

We forget that, to most young Chinese, the Cultural Revolution of 1966–76 is about as distant and foreign as the French Revolution is to the young of France. Mao and Deng are ancient history to this generation, as far removed in the imagination as the emperors of distant dynasties like

Qin Shi Huang and Qianlong. The young Chinese of today are the beneficiaries of an extraordinary shift within two generations towards middle-income prosperity. There is enormous pressure to do well in secondary school so that you can enter a good university, or perhaps, if your family can afford it, to study overseas—although to our great cost, Australia is now off the list for many Chinese students. Confucian ethics place education as central to advancement in life. And even if some of these young people don't like aspects of their motherland, they feel an attachment to it. They applaud the nation's success, they are immensely proud of its rise in world affairs, and they embrace a proper, shared patriotism, as they should. If Chinese students in Australia have shared these attitudes, that does not make them stooges for China, let alone a threat to Australia, as some have suggested.

FINDING OUR WAY OUT OF THE FOREST

I have been critical of our government in this book because it lacks the sophistication and wisdom to handle these challenging times and to stand up for a more far-sighted and modern Australia. I know that I will be criticised for this. I have said that there is much to be critical of in Chinese policy and behaviour, but I have not set out to detail this because so many others are banging this drum. I said that our Prime Minister should be asking how we can make the relationship with China better, pointing to the need for a more independent foreign policy, respectful of but distinctly separate from that of the United States. I would now like to make a few modest suggestions about the steps we might consider to help us emerge from this dark and threatening forest and take the path back towards improved relations with China.

In my role as cultural counsellor, I negotiated the loan of two giant pandas as China's birthday present to mark the celebration of Australia's Bicentenary in 1988. For two years, I met monthly with my counterparts from the Ministry of Forestry and Fisheries, who had responsibility for making the necessary arrangements on the Chinese side. I used to call these 'three teapot meetings'; career diplomats might call them 'full and frank discussions'. We would cover an immense amount of detail on matters such as transport, security, insurance, feeding, facilities at the Australian zoos, quarantine and veterinary requirements, travel and living arrangements for the animals' keepers, and, of course, fees, where the Chinese side wanted a very big sum for sharing the pandas.

The Chinese are masterful negotiators—in this, they only really respect as equals the Japanese, who share an understanding of this ancient art—but I learned quickly, resisting what I regarded as over-the-top 'rent a panda' terms and regularly retreating to another cup of tea, talk of 'friendship between our two great leaders' and/or 'two great peoples', and the obvious line that it was not appropriate to be offered a birthday gift and then be presented with the bill. We started each meeting focusing on areas where we could find agreement, working through issues carefully, point by point. Then, when we came to a stumbling block and could not find common ground in regards to a particular clause, we would put that issue aside, have yet another cup of tea, talk about friendship, and agree to meet again the following month.

And so it went, month by month, until the Melbourne and Sydney zoos, which had each invested over $1 million to build new enclosures, grow the appropriate bamboos and import huge amounts of panda merchandise for their shops, panicked, upon which both the ambassador and I received a steady stream of Australian Government instructions to sign up. I refused to accept what I thought were unreasonable terms, and the ambassador trusted my judgement. I tried to reassure the Australian parties that there was absolutely no chance that the pandas would not arrive on schedule, because this had been agreed by the two leaders at the time—prime minister Bob Hawke and premier Zhao Ziyang—plus it had been widely publicised, and so a serious issue of 'face' was involved.

Then, after predicting that negotiations would go right to the door of the plane sent to collect the pandas, my term in Beijing finished and I came home. My successor as cultural counsellor, Dr Nicholas Jose, subsequently told me that, in fact, the toing and froing had gone beyond that moment because, when the Qantas jumbo pulled up to load the pandas, the Chinese determined that it was inappropriate for their national animal to be pictured waving goodbye beside the Qantas logo of the flying kangaroo. At the very last moment, they switched the loading to an Air China plane, the photographers took their pictures, and the pandas then took off with their own national carrier, flying to Tokyo where they were reloaded onto the Qantas aircraft.

The lessons here are pretty obvious. Don't be offended by sudden changes—both sides have domestic electorates to which they play all the time. Be curious and try to understand the case from the other's point of view. Deals reached at the highest levels of government are given the highest level of respect, as serious national 'face' has been invested in them and the word of the leader must be honoured. When Australia says it wants to hold meetings at the highest level of government to sort things out, it really does not help at all for our PM to play 'Macho Man' when a little humility and large dollops of courtesy would go a lot further. Clear and positive objectives, consistency of values, a polite firmness, genuine sincerity and patience are very important in all dealings.

Furthermore, negotiations will be far more productive if you start with those areas where you are likely to find agreement and can build trust. There are many possibilities here for Australia: sporting and cultural exchanges; joint medical and agricultural research; even, dare I say it, climate change action, on which Australia is the laggard. There might be joint aid projects in some Pacific and Asian countries that are in both Australia and China's national interest—for example, promoting the education of women. But for now, Australia needs to put to one side the more difficult issues. And we need to learn that chest thumping and megaphone diplomacy are entirely counterproductive, especially when we are using someone else's megaphone.

The Chinese people's sense of time is also very different to ours. They have a much longer time horizon and vastly greater patience in working towards a desired outcome. In 1986, when I accompanied Barry Jones to that rocket-launching base in Xichang, we were taken out to a scenic Buddhist temple above a remote mountain lake. Suddenly, speedboats came roaring into view, pulling a group of waterskiers. I turned to our military host to ask what the waterskiers were doing in this out-of-the-way location. 'They are training for the Olympics,' he said, matter-of-factly. I replied with the obvious retort that waterskiing was not an Olympic sport. 'Ahhh,' my host said thoughtfully, 'that is right. But when it is, China will be ready.'

Long-term strategic plans and the necessary investment to achieve them are crucial. China sets ambitious, far-sighted national goals and works hard to fulfil them. Australia, however, thinks in short electoral cycles, and our politicians are motivated more by the desire to attract votes at the next election and retain their perks of office than any long-term national benefit (although they always try very hard to dress the former in the language of the latter). This leads to a lack of discipline as individual politicians try to differentiate themselves or score points. Our adversarial parliamentary system means that 'wining' today's domestic media cycle has become the most important objective for both government and Opposition. The very best thing most Australian politicians can do to improve relations with China is simply to shut up.

There are many problems with a centralised autocracy, but its strengths include discipline down the line and an ability to focus on the definition and delivery of national goals. There are lessons we can learn here from China. I think of the extraordinary development of infrastructure of every kind across the country in the past few decades. Tullamarine Airport opened in Melbourne in July 1970. At that time, we were promised that a fast train would soon run from the airport into the city. For fifty years now, successive governments have continued to tell us it is coming soon, but we don't even have a slow tram doing the 23-kilometre trip. In the last twenty years, China has built almost 40 000 kilometres of fast-train tracks and countless huge new stations, and high-speed trains carry many millions of people across the country every day.

IT'S TIME TO REBUILD TRUST

Travelling back from Xichang to Chengdu on an overnight train, I was sitting having a drink with our minders from the State Science and Technology Commission for Defence. One of them asked me how I was enjoying my time as a diplomat. I said that I really loved being in China, that the people were friendly, the job constantly different and stimulating, but I added that after a life in the theatre, I was struggling to come to terms with being treated as a spy—having my phones tapped; my movements watched; occasionally being conscious of being followed in the street; watching the cook making notes of who came to dinner, notes he would then submit to the Diplomatic Service Bureau. Initially my minders said, 'Oh no, that couldn't happen here,' but as I gave more examples, they laughed and started telling me of their own experiences when posted as science counsellors in various Chinese embassies abroad. A small story from that night stays with me: one day, in a kitchen in the lower bowels of the Chinese Embassy in Washington, DC, the head chef cut his hand very badly with a knife—an ambulance was there before anyone present could make the call. Be assured that America, even our own beloved Australia, plays the same games, so we need to avoid hypocrisy in our political posturing. It's not just those tricky communists who bug embassies and foreign governments, or use facial-recognition technologies. Indeed, we probably all shop with the same Israeli suppliers.

If we are going to condemn what we see as human rights violations and internal repression in China, let's acknowledge that it is no more of a threat to the international order than many other global examples. Let's be consistent and invest the same energy condemning India, Belarus, Vietnam, Saudi Arabia, Cambodia and Myanmar. Let's deal with human rights issues here in Australia, too, specifically Indigenous disadvantage and the scandalous treatment of asylum seekers. If we are going to talk about prison populations, let's not just talk about Xinjiang but also about the shocking incarceration rates of blacks in the United States.

It is time to start rebuilding trust. It's time, as former prime minister Paul Keating said, for Australia to find its security *within* our own region rather than *from* our region through dependence on our US protector. Our long-term prosperity and security depend on good relations across our region, not on an erratic and distant ally focused on its own interests and with a history of dragging us into futile wars. Many years ago, another Australian prime minister, the conservative Malcom Fraser, warned us of the dangers of attaching ourselves too securely to the Americans. And if I might close with a prime ministerial trifecta, I recall that our previous PM, Malcom Turnbull, offended China mightily when he misquoted Mao Zedong—referring to the foreign interference legislation to address what he saw as Chinese meddling in Australia, he said, 'The Australian people have stood up.'

I only wish we would.

ACKNOWLEDGEMENTS

I thank my wife Ziyin for her deep sensitivity and her capacity both to bridge and to connect utterly different cultures so successfully; I thank her family for welcoming me into their world; and I thank David Ambrose, former DFAT officer and minister at the Australian Embassy in Beijing during my term there as cultural counsellor, for his informed comments and his permission to draw on thinking from his unpublished notes.

I have learned something from so many good people in my life, and there is always much more to learn.

This book is based on the University of Adelaide Kidman Lecture delivered on 17 July 2021 as part of the Adelaide Festival of Ideas.

NOTES

1   Department of Foreign Affairs and Trade, 'China Country Brief', 2021, https://www.dfat.gov.au/geo/china/china-country-brief (viewed 4 November 2021).

2   Both quotations from Vijay Gokhale, 'China's Vision of Hegemony: The View from India', *Regional Security Outlook 2021*, Council for Security Cooperation in the Asia Pacific—reprinted as an edited version on John Menadue's *Pearls and Irritations* website.

3   Robert Gottliebsen, *The Australian*, 18 March 2021 and 25 May 2021.